Snodland
in old picture postcards

Dr. Andrew Ashbee

 European Library ZALTBOMMEL/THE NETHERLANDS

GB ISBN 90 288 6651 5

© 2001 European Library – Zaltbommel/The Netherlands
      Snodland Historical Society

European Library
post office box 49
NL – 5300 AA Zaltbommel/The Netherlands
telephone: 0031 418 513144
fax: 0031 418 515515
e-mail:publisher@eurobib.nl

Introduction

Early forms of the name 'Snodilande, Snoddingland, Snodingeland' lead scholars to suggest that it derives from a person called Snodd or Snodda. There is plenty of evidence to show continuous occupation here from the late Bronze Age to the present day. A prehistoric ring ditch, a Saxon cemetery, a Roman villa and tumulus and ninth-century charters all precede the Domesday survey. Snodland is sited at a point where the river Medway cuts through the North Downs, providing flood-free settlement for early man. Streams for drinking water, meadow, arable and woodland were all near at hand. A river crossing was established and the Medway also provided easy communication up and down stream.

Snodland remained a typical small agricultural community until the nineteenth century, but its size and character then changed enormously with the development of the paper and cement industries. A paper mill was operating from at least the 1730s and commercial limeburners from about 1819, but it was not until the 1850s that the two industries expanded markedly: the coming of the railway in 1856 had much to do with this. The population of Snodland in 1801 was 312, in 1851 was 617 and in 1901 was 3091. A further boost in size has occurred since the 1950s and the population today is estimated at around 12,000 and growing.

Parishioners will be among the first to acknowledge that Snodland is not a pretty place. There are now very few buildings which pre-date the expansion of the mid-nineteenth century. A pressing need between 1850 and 1950 was to provide homes for workmen in the factories, so the bulk of the town landscape is of rows of terraced houses from this time. To these a number of large housing estates have been added in recent years. With the advent of the car Snodland is now conveniently situated between two motorways and many commute to work elsewhere as work opportunities in the local factories have declined. Yet if one looks carefully there are attractive areas and the casual traveller passing through the town would be surprised to find that a large part of the west of the parish is still beautiful farm and down land. The hamlets of Paddlesworth and Holborough retain a historic atmosphere through their groups of ancient buildings.

On the whole this selection of photographs is concerned with places rather than people. Among the latter John May (1734-1805) was the principal parishioner in the eighteenth century, establishing two charities and serving the community in many ways. Thomas Fletcher Waghorn (1800-1850), although born in Chatham, belonged to a local family, lived in Snodland in later life and is buried in the churchyard. He established the Overland Route to India via Egypt and worked tirelessly to speed up transmission of people and mail between England and India. The Hook family came to Snodland from Gloucestershire in the 1850s. It was Charles Townsend Hook (1831-1877) who successfully built up the paper mill – it still bears his name today. The family were very generous in providing many facilities for the community: school, clock tower, public baths, coffee tavern and pavilion feature among innumerable smaller charitable acts. William Lee (1801-1881) bought the lime works in 1846, which also prospered; it passed through his descendants and was acquired by APCM in 1931.

The views in 'old' photographs of Snodland are not appreciably different from those of today, the greatest exception being the absence of cars and traffic. There are relatively few photographs currently known which date from before 1900 – most are school groups and personal photographs. But from around 1904 there is a rich choice, thanks particularly to the efforts of Arthur Nethersole Hambrook, a local stationer, who supplied a constant stream of images for nearly fifty years. Smaller selections were provided by William Bateman, postmaster 1906-1909, and R. Mason and Sons circa 1905-1910. To samples of these we have added a few paintings and non-commercial photographs supplied by individuals.

Andrew Ashbee

Acknowledgements

All pictures are taken from copies or originals in the collection of Snodland Historical Society. The late Gerald Edgeler spent a life-time collecting local photographs and we have drawn extensively on his examples. We also thank the late L. Jefferys, Mr. John Soane, Mr. William Wenham and the Snodland and Ham Hill Women's Institute for supplying other items.

Bibliography

Ashbee, Andrew: *A Little History of Snodland* 1994.
Wall, Rev. Charles de Rocfort: *Snodland and its History 55 B.C. to A.D. 1928* 1928 (abridged reprint as Snodland Historical Society pamphlet No. 13. 2000)
Woolmer, J.: *Historical Jottings of the Parish of Snodland* 1894 (reprinted as Snodland Historical Society pamphlet No. 3. 1998)
Snodland Historical Society pamphlets (details at www.snodlandhistory.org.uk)

1   The parish church of All Saints' is Snodland's oldest building and it has been a familiar landmark at the east end of the High Street from time immemorial. It is likely that a church has stood on this site since Saxon times and it is certainly mentioned in the Domesday Book. The earliest parts of the present building are Norman, including the centre of the west wall here peeping over the trees. Some Roman building materials robbed from a villa which stood a little to the north can also be seen in the walls. Most of the fabric dates from the 13th century, however, with aisles, west porch and the impressive tower added in the 14th and 15th centuries. On the west wall the lines of the roof before the two aisles were added are still visible. Much of the foliage in this view of circa 1905 has disappeared, allowing the building to be seen more easily.

2 The massive tower of All Saints' Church includes a priest's room on the first floor, no doubt abandoned in favour of a rectory after the Reformation. It may have served as the village lock-up in later times. The clock was installed in 1849. This photograph seems to date from 1881 or soon after, for the foundations in the foreground are of the Court Lodge barn destroyed by fire on 11 July that year. The wind spread the flames to the parish church: the Rector noted 'the wooden shutter window in the belfry was on fire, the bell chamber covered with burning straw, burning straw on the roof and the notice board on the Church burning and charred'. Buckets were carried by hand up to the belfry and all was saved. The barn belonged to Silas Peters (1853-1914), son of Thomas William Peters (c.1817-1905), the village coal merchant, who can be seen in his carriage beside the church gate. He built Anchor Place in the High Street in 1860, having previously lived at Holborough. The large cross was erected in 1846 on the me-

diaeval stones of the old market place, moved here from outside the Red Lion by the Rector, Henry Dampier Phelps.

3　This interior view of All Saints' Church was probably taken soon after the completion of renovations in 1905. It certainly dates from before 1909, when the organ was replaced by the present instrument and the window visible between the right-hand pillars was converted into the vestry doorway. The unique mediaeval crucifix on the pillar was rediscovered during nineteenth-century renovations. The mural above the chancel arch was painted in 1879, but was covered over about fifty years ago. The floor of the chancel and sanctuary are lower in this picture. They were raised to their present height in 1913. The east window shows four Protestant martyrs (Anne Ayscough, Nicholas Ridley, Hugh Latimer and Thomas Cranmer) and was installed by Rev. Henry Dampier Phelps, around 1845-1846. Like much of the church glass it was destroyed by a near-by land mine on 21 February 1941. Phelps was Rector for 61 years – 1804-1865 – and recorded £1,644. 5s. spent during his incumbency to maintain and preserve the ancient fabric.

All Saints' Church, Snodland.

4 An artist's view of Christ Church, printed on the collecting boxes for donations towards its erection. The boxes also include a message from the Vicar of Birling, 5 March 1891, telling of the need for the church: 'Owing to the rapid increase of the inhabitants at the north-east end of Birling, adjoining Snodland, that part of the Parish has grown from a population of fifty to upwards of seven hundred, with the certain prospect of a still further growth. This is due to the proximity of the Cement, Brick and Paper Works, which have lately been largely augmented. ... The cost of it, including Tower, will be £2,350. ... This District is inhabited entirely by the Working Classes, and none of the principal owners of property are resident within it, or able to assist much.'

5 Work on building Christ Church was begun on 1 March 1892 and the foundation stone was laid by Hon. Mrs. Ralph Nevill of Birling on 30 April that year. The church, which was designed by Percy Monckton in Early English style, was built by Robert Langridge, a builder from Ham Hill. A tower was planned (as shown in picture 4), but was never built, either because of lack of funds, or fear of unstable foundations. Church and churchyard were consecrated by the Bishop of Dover on 10 October 1893. Initially clergy were supplied by the mother church of Birling, but on 8 November 1908, Rev. A. Pollok Williams took particular responsibility for Christ Church. A separate parish was created by Order in Council of 23 January 1911. This postcard was issued just prior to Rev. Williams' institution and induction on 12 May.

Christ Church. Malling Road, Snodland.

Rev. A. P. Williams, Vicar. New Parish of Lower Birling.

6   Rev. A Pollok Williams was well-known too as a sportsman. Here he is, third from right in the back row of Snodland Institute Football Club in the 1910-1911 season. The trophies are not specified, but the shield seems to be the Maidstone Hospital Charity Shield, which appears in several photographs of various Snodland teams over the years. Rev. Williams also played cricket and bowls, the latter at County standard, and he also ran a boxing club for boys. In 1921 he moved to All Hallows, Hoo, and eventually was made a Canon. Most of the other people in the photograph can be identified.

Second from left in the back row is Joshua Wilford (c.1856-1931), well-known as a local builder, lay preacher and undertaker. His son Joshua (1886-1936) has the ball.

7   An ancient ferry ran from Halling to Wouldham, but there is no record of a ferry at Snodland until the nineteenth century. It is marked on the tithe map of 1844. An agreement was made on 28 May 1853 between Edward Baker, ferryman, and the Earl of Aylesford, giving Baker the right to land his passengers on either side of the river at an annual rent of one guinea. However, the Rector of Snodland owned Glebe land on the Snodland side and also demanded a rent. On 20 August 1874, after much hard bargaining, the Rector persuaded Baker that the annual rent due to him should be increased from £20 to £30. Baker clearly made a good living, because he was able to build a grand house – Nephalite Villa – at the top of the High Street (seen in picture No. 11). At this time newspapers record that 600 people a day were using the service to and from the various factories on either bank. Many of these closed in the 1920s and 1930s and the ferry itself ceased in 1948, having for some years been managed by the Stevens family. This picture dates from about 1905.

THE FERRY, SNODLAND, KENT.

8 Many of the local factories moved bulk materials such as cement and paper pulp by water. Medway barges with their distinctive red sails were a common sight from the mid-nineteenth century onwards and firms such as Townsend Hook and Associated Portland Cement Company at Snodland had their own vessels. One can be seen in the distance here, with the company emblem on the sail. The barges were usually manned by a captain and his mate (sometimes two). In time the practice grew up of towing a string of barges by steam tug. Here an unidentified tug has just negotiated the great horse-shoe bend at Snodland and is passing the ferry with its barges in tow, lashed two abreast.

River Medway from Haymen's Wharf, Snodland. Hambrook's Photo Series.

9 The Rectory built by Thomas Dampier Phelps (Rector 1804-1865) in 1814 replaced an earlier building further to the east (near where the Water Company offices are today). When Rev. Carey became Rector in 1865 he enlarged and extensively rebuilt it. Some of the rooms were enormous – 'the drawing room 24 ft x 20 ft and the dining room 20 ft x 16 ft' (as was the bedroom above). Not surprisingly later residents found it extremely cold! The photograph shows the front entrance porch. Next to the house was the stable (for three horses) and a coach house (for two coaches) was furthest to the right. The Rectory was often a centre for village life and many fêtes were held here. All the buildings were demolished in 1969 following the joining of All Saints' and Christ Church parishes and the Rector now lives in the more practical vicarage which formerly belonged to Christ Church. Rectory Close now occupies the site of this building.

Snodland Rectory.

10 A long private avenue ran from the High Street south to the Rectory, as seen on this photograph of circa 1905. The cricket meadow beyond the right-hand line of trees was formerly Glebe land belonging to the Rector, but was given to the parish for recreational use by Rev. Charles de Rocfort Wall in 1909. The lower end of this avenue has been used as the basis for the car park. In 1865 Rev. Carey arrived to find two disputes regarding ownership of trees on his boundaries. One concerning those on the far side of the cricket meadow was resolved amicably, but the other resulted in a court case and he was distressed that he was ordered to cut down twelve trees on the west side of Rectory Avenue. Others were planted as replacements once the boundaries were defined, but most have now gone — swallowed up by the necessity for a car park.

Rectory Avenue, Snodland, Kent.

11 This view of the High Street dates from around 1905. Durham House (extreme left) belonged to the coal merchant, while the row of shops beyond was in place by 1891. Today several still retain their original trades: corn shop, shoes (tobacconist and draper have gone), stationer, baker. Opposite a horse-chestnut tree stood in the little garden belonging to the grocer/butcher on the corner – familiar to older residents as The World Stores. At the time of the photograph this was owned by the Bateman family and William Bateman also ran the post office next door, part of 'Nephalite Villa'

mentioned at picture 7. Sitting in his trap outside is William George Collins, who carried the post between Snodland and Rochester. Collins was a celebrated figure in Snodland

and when he retired on 14 November 1908 a postcard was issued in commemoration. He had only one arm, but built his own house (still in Queen's Avenue), taking ten years. The card

states that over forty years he travelled 298,300 miles on his postal duties.

High Street, Snodland, Kent.

12   Apart from the absence of cars, this view east down the High Street has changed little since the photograph was taken around 1905. Sideways on, in the distance, with a traction engine alongside, were Gorham's Cottages, a group of four houses built in the early 1800s. They were demolished some years ago because they obstructed the path and road. The Congregational Church (now the United Church) was opened on 28 November 1888 by the celebrated preacher, Rev. Charles Spurgeon, from Greenwich. It cost £1,531. 15s. 0d. of which £1,050 was realized by the sale of the previous chapel in Holborough Road. The large houses facing the cricket meadow were among the grandest in Snodland and included a doctor's surgery and the manse for the New Church opposite.

HIGH St SNODLAND.
(SHOWING CONGREGATIONAL CHURCH)

13 Snodland post office had three different locations before it was housed in the present building, erected in 1909. The first was on the site of the New Jerusalem Church, the second was on the corner of May Street and the High Street, the third (as seen in picture 11) was on the north side of the High Street (now replaced by a supermarket). Early postmasters usually combined the job with other work, such as schoolmaster or overseer. One of them, Walter Rumble, absconded with £270. 15s. 11d of parish funds in 1880, but his wife and son were apparently not blamed for this offence and continued to run the post office for some years afterwards! Here the staff pose for the camera at the opening, with Mr. Horace Verrall, the postmaster, in a straw hat. The offices of Argles and Court, solicitors, are at the left. It was they who had arranged the sale of the land for the new building from the church estates. As Snodland increased in size it eventually became necessary for the post office to expand into the whole building.

14 The first doctor to reside in Snodland was Charles White in 1869. He set up his home and surgery in what is now called May Place, near the station. For the previous sixteen years Dr. White had worked on Peninsular & Orient steamers, so he called his home 'Nyanza House' after the ship he sailed in. He retired in 1887 and was replaced by Dr. John Palmer (c.1852-1914). Dr. Palmer was one of the first people in Snodland to own a motor car and there are two photographs of him outside the surgery sitting in his vehicles with his driver, E. Ensal. D 439 was replaced by the larger D 4478 shown in the present picture. It is a Rover 8 h.p., single cylinder, chain-driven vehicle. On the reverse of the card is printed 'Xmas, 1910, New-Year, 1911. With Best Wishes for a Bright and Happy Christmas and a Glad and Prosperous New Year, from J. Palmer', but it is rumoured that only those who had paid their bills received the card!

15 The construction of the Snodland by-pass, opened in 1983, has substantially altered the view west from the church tower compared with this scene, perhaps dating from the 1920s. There is now no direct route for vehicles traversing the High Street, which is cut in two by the by-pass a few yards beyond the position of the horse and cart in the picture. Other changes are relatively minor. The little railway gatehouse – home to railway employees since the route was opened – has gone. The signalman no longer has to manipulate the gates by hand, but has a covered way to his wheel leading from the signal box. The neat gardens beside the Queen's Hotel later became two sidings, but are now overgrown and the hotel itself has become a residential home.

High Street, Snodland from Church Tower.

A.N. HAMBROOK, SNODLAND.

16   Until the advent of the car, the High Street was busy with pedestrian traffic to and from the railway, the ferry, the paper mill and other industrial places of work. Such activity is not much in evidence in this quiet view, which William Bateman caught with his camera about 1906-1909. The Queen's Hotel was erected in 1856, at the same time as the railway, and was well-placed to receive visitors. In early days it was often the venue for parish meetings of various kinds. Alongside the doctor's surgery on the right were shops catering for the passer-by: sweets, tobacconist and stationers and one or two cafés. Now these have all become houses, while others further to the west, both in the High Street and in Brook Street, were demolished to make way for the by-pass.

SNODLAND, KENT.   W. BATEMAN, POST OFFICE, SNODLAND.

17   After they acquired ownership of the paper mill, the Hook family moved to Snodland from Tovil in 1854. They took up residence in 'Acacia Cottage' in the High Street, an old house which had been home to several paper mill managers before them. In the 1860s they replaced 'Acacia Cottage' with this impressive house, photographed in 1929. They named it 'Veles' after the ancient manor of this part of Snodland – a name derived in turn from the family 'Vel/Veel/Vitele', resident here from the 1200s. The original manor house beside All Saints' was by this time in a decrepit state.

In 1864 a chapel seating eighty persons was built within 'Veles'; the entrance doorway can be seen at the near end.

18 Before they came to Snodland the Hook family had embraced the teachings of the Swedish intellectual Emanuel Swedenborg (1688-1772) and, together with some of their workforce who came with them, they formed a Society of the Swedenborgian Church in Snodland. At first meetings were held in a cottage and then in 'Veles', but after some difficulty finding a site, they purchased one in the High Street in 1882 – even though this required the demolition of several properties. The builder was 'Mr. H. Bridge of Maidstone' and the foundation stone was laid on 11 November 1881 by Agnes Hook, the youngest daughter, deputizing for her ill mother, who died nine days later. The church was dedicated on 27 June 1882 and was subsequently called 'St John the Evangelist (Church of the New Jerusalem)'. The building remained in use for more than 100 years, but following closure and sale, services have since returned again to homes, just as in the earliest days.

Church of the New Jerusalem
Snodland

19 Maude Midsummer Hook, the last of the family, died at Hove on 29 September 1930, aged 90. 'Veles' was subsequently demolished and a row of eight houses called 'Veles Gardens' was built on the site. They can be seen at the centre right of this photograph which dates from about 1950. In the 1980s it was their turn to be demolished, since they were on the route of the by-pass (completed in 1983). Other victims of this development were Pierce and Baldwin's grocer's shop (which had served as such since at least 1840), the Victory public house next door and the baker's beyond. In the eighteenth century this group was the site of the village poorhouses ('old' and 'new') – where the destitute of the parish were placed before the rise of the Union workhouses – and other old buildings.

High Street, Snodland.

A.N. Hambrook
High St. Snodland.

20　When 'Veles' was demolished in 1930 the paper mill took the opportunity to build additional houses on the site for their employees. As well as 'Veles Gardens' shown in the previous picture, others were built around the garden perimeter: five in May Street and another five in Brook Street. The latter replaced this lovely old thatched house – 'Sweetbriar Cottage'. The last resident was Margaret Viney. She is seen at the gate in 1926, photographed by Sidney Storkey, whose drug stores were opposite. The earliest known reference to this building is a deed of 1613, which shows it then had a barn, garden, orchards and other land attached to it.

21　On Sunday 12 August 1906 the worst catastrophe to affect the village was the total destruction by fire of the paper mill. Four hundred men were thrown out of work for two years and thirty-one families were evacuated from their houses (although twelve of these were soon able to return). The fire began when a paraffin lamp ignited a rope during repair work. Fire Brigades from Snodland, Halling, Malling, Maidstone, Rochester and Chatham were unable to contain the fire that destroyed two barges as well as 5-6 acres of buildings. One curiosity was that an 'iron frame of one of the large sheds had been in two fires. It was part of the Crystal Palace, and after the fire there was purchased by Colonel Holland and put up here. The girders and standards are still intact, though somewhat bent by the heat'. (We have not discovered details about a Crystal Palace fire prior to 1906.)

No 4 Paper Machine.

412

22 The Kent Messenger reported: 'It is the mill that represents loss and ruin, but the pathos of it all is most vividly realized when one returns to the cottages and the churchyard. Some of the upper rooms are absolutely denuded of their windows, and the rooms themselves are empty. Downstairs one sees furniture of all kinds crowded promiscuously into one confused heap. In the churchyard are fragments of crockery, broken ornaments, dresses, mattresses, chairs, washing stands and all sort of domestic utensils, unusable, abandoned, showing the panic with which they were tumbled out – anywhere away from the fire. The dispossessed cottagers come and sadly survey these remnants of their goods, and search for that which they cannot find, and prompt as were the steps taken for their assistance by a provisional Committee, many must suffer the loss of goods rashly precipitated from the tenements by thoughtless but well-meaning persons.'

23 Fortunately the paper mill was fully insured and the order books had been saved, so it was determined that 'as many of the mill-men as circumstances permit will be employed on the work that is immediately possible'. Nevertheless the whole community suffered from these straightened circumstances and a number of Snodland families emigrated at this time, especially to Canada, America and the Antipodes. The mill was rebuilt by 1908 resulting in the familiar large blocks of buildings alongside the railway. These covered the former entrance in Mill Street and the properties leading up to it, but have in turn become redundant, with most of the mill's current activity occurring elsewhere on the site.

THE NEW PAPER MILL, SNODLAND.
(FROM THE BROOK)

24 There are several variant issues of this photograph, but it is only recently that we have been able to date it with any accuracy. The rebuilding of the paper mill was completed in 1908 and it appears the picture was taken soon afterwards, for a copy postmarked 1909 has come to light. The seven boys had probably finished school for the day (the factory clock shows 4.30 p.m.) and were certainly curious to observe the cameraman at work. Church Field was not only a field, but also the name given to an ancient footpath leading to Holborough. It was diverted a little when the railway was built and some of the houses here at the south end are among the earliest remaining in the village. The elaborate one second on the left is 'Sunnyside', the home of Joshua Wilford at one time, and now, much modified although still recognizable, is called 'Fleet House'.

Church Fields Snodland.

Hambrook's Photo Series.

25 The National Schools in Brook Street were the oldest in the parish. William Lewis, the parish clerk, set up a school in his house on this site in 1762. Between 1793 and Lewis' death in 1797 tax returns refer to it as the 'free school', so evidently some kind of benefaction was then in place. In 1800 the local squire, John May, set up a charity to supply a schoolmaster, who was required to teach twenty poor children from Snodland and ten each from Halling and Birling. Others would have to pay. The building in the photograph was begun in 1867 and enlarged in the 1870s under a new charitable trust. But around 1904, when this picture was taken, the school's income was 18s. 7d. a quarter, out of which the building had to be kept in repair! The Charity Commissioners came to the rescue and in 1948 the school came under the control of Kent Education Committee. With the impending construction of the Snodland bypass a new school was built in Roberts Road and this one closed on 26 November 1979.

...l Schools. Snodland. Published by A. N. Hambrook, Printer and Station r, Snodland

26 Some older parishioners will recognize this interior view of the National Schools in Brook Street, for this area daily served as dining room as well as class rooms. Originally it was the boys' part of the school. This picture is said to date from around 1905. The headmaster, Mr. Charles Godfrey, is seated at his desk, with F. Miller alongside. At the piano is Mr. J. Cuthbert, with Frank Austin standing. The name of the monitor on the right is unknown. It is likely that many of the items on the walls are those given when the school was enlarged in 1868 – the pictures by Mrs. Anne Roberts of Holborough and the maps by Rev. Thomas P. Phelps, Rector of Ridley (nephew of Thomas Dampier Phelps, Rector of Snodland, who had died three years earlier). The row of rifles was of no concern in those far-off days! They probably belonged to the local Volunteers.

27   An old footpath leads on from what was the south end of Brook Street, although today it is much altered by the business park and new access to the lake. The tithe map of 1844 already shows a neat, straight path lined with trees and it is quite likely that this was made in the eighteenth century. Parishioners called part of it 'Willow Walk'. The willow trees were said to be of particularly high quality for making cricket bats, and from time to time a tree was felled for this purpose. It was a delightful spot, as is shown by the picture. The Brook through which the path still passes was the common meadow land for the parish, originally comprising some 80 acres. Parts were leased to the paper mill. Parishioners had a right to turn out cattle on it, subject to certain restrictions of time and numbers.

28 The railway through Snodland opened in 1856 and helped bring great prosperity to the village. Charles Townsend Hook realized its potential value when he purchased the paper mill two years earlier. All the local industries, especially the paper-making and cement factories, made great use of it and in the days before most people had their own cars it carried many of their workers too and from their homes. Times have changed. The staff smartly lining the platform as the train departs in this picture of around 1905 have no modern counterparts, for the station is unmanned. The once busy goods shed and its attendant sidings have long gone. Trains to London are now timetabled to take ten minutes longer than they were in 1873!

29 One of the few old buildings to have survived in Snodland is 'Mulberry Cottage' in the High Street, so called because of a mulberry tree in the garden. It appears to have been a typical fifteenth-century Kentish hall-house, but no records of it are known until around 1600. In the eighteenth century it was the home of the Manley family, who were maltsters making the local beer, and for a time there was an oast house attached. John Manley died a bankrupt in 1797 and the property was auctioned. His widow was allowed to live in part of the house until her death in 1822, but shared it with two other households. In time it became three shops as is shown in this photograph. The far end had been a blacksmith's for many years (beginning with Matthew Tong), with the smithy behind, and the centre shop belonged to Horatio Draycon, plumber. In the distance is the 'British Schools Manual Training Classroom' erected in 1893 by the Misses Hook as an adjunct to the British Schools in Holborough Road – only the second in the county – where the senior boys were taught woodwork.

Old Houses, High Street, Snodland

30   In 1932 Mulberry Cottage was given by the paper mill to the Dedrick Memorial Pension Fund (founded in memory of William Dedrick (d.1920), a former manager of the mill). The whole building was stripped to a skeleton, the nineteenth-century accretions were removed and today it probably looks much as it did when first built (although now divided into two properties). The stone 'moat' and gate were all added at this time. Originally the house had 6-7 acres of land, some around and behind it and the rest as small fields on the opposite side of the High Street. The interior has been completely changed; where once there seem to have been three low stories there are now only two.

Old Houses High Street, Snodland

A.H. HAMBROOK
High St. Snodland.

31 The Devonshire Rooms in Waghorn Road were built in 1895 by Agnes and Maude Midsummer Hook. The previous year they had written 'A Few Recollections of our Summer in Devonshire: a Letter read to the quarterly meeting of the Snodland (New Church) Society, October 30th, 1894', so perhaps this is why the name was chosen. The New Church Sunday School met here, but it was always intended too as a place for village meetings. It remains a hive of activity for many Snodland societies and clubs and is also available for private functions. In recent years the offices of Snodland Town Council have occupied the space which once served for the caretaker's lodgings. Alongside are two sets of almshouses, now housing ten tenants, also the gift of the two sisters. The nearest was in memory of their brother Eustace (d. 1890), opened on 27 December 1893; the other, in memory of their governess Amelia Drummond, was opened in 1903.

Devonshire Rooms, Waghorn Road, Snodland.

32 Here is another of William Bateman's photographs, taken about 1905-1909. The Bull Hotel on the left replaced an earlier building, pulled down on 10 February 1881. Study of the 1868 and 1897 Ordnance Survey maps suggests that the new building occupies the site of former outbuildings, probably stables, and that the earlier 'Bull' was behind them to the west. Precise positions are blurred because the road was widened at the same time. Part of Bateman's grocer's and butcher's shops are on the right, with T.J. Moore's ironmonger's beyond. Albert Norman's butcher's shop is half-hidden by foliage and the Working Men's Institute is in the distance. Perhaps the horse-drawn carriage belongs to Robert Ashby of Halling.

SNODLAND, KENT.

W. BATEMAN, POST OFFICE, SNODLAND.

33 We can be sure that A.N. Hambrook was on hand to capture the moment when the first motor bus serving a route from Chatham to West Malling via Strood and Snodland ran on 15 March 1920. Older parishioners tell of a little chocolate bus (the one in the photograph) costing 1½d for children and 3d for adults to West Malling. Mr. Sand ran an orange bus costing 1s 3d return fare to Chatham. The bus is passing what finally became 'The World Stores', grocers, before it was demolished to make way for a modern supermarket, although a 1740 map calls it 'The Old Bull'. The building was certainly of great antiquity, but there is no known link with the 'Bull Hotel' opposite. This cross-roads has been the centre of Snodland for a hundred years or so, but before that the middle of the village was sited at the Red Lion and the junction of Brook Street and the High Street.

Holborough Road, Snodland. (Showing New Motor Bus) Hambrook's Photo Series.

34   This view of Holborough Road has changed relatively little over the past hundred years. Albert Norman's butcher's shop on the left is now occupied by other traders. Beyond this is the entrance to Lee Road – an unmade surface – which at the time had no houses. On the extreme right is the front of the 'Bricklayers Arms', part of an extended set of properties owned and built by the Moore family. John Moore (1802-1858) was the first of the family to move to Snodland, living at first in a small timbered house (remembered in more recent times as Baldock's electrical shop). He and his sons were bricklayers, but later became grocers and butchers.

They prospered, adding a substantial ironmonger's premises on the south side and the 'Bricklayer's Arms' on the north; presumably the latter got its name because of their former profession. Today it has been replaced by Ostler's Court. Beyond is the parade, with its unusual Dutch-style upper storeys.

Holborough Road, Snodland.

Hambrook's, Photo Series.

35   On 23 March 1912 the Snodland Picture Palace cinema opened in Holborough Road. Later known as the Grand and then the Queens, it had 360 seats. Children were admitted for 2d (including popcorn). Prices at the box office in the photograph show 3d, 4d, 6d, and 8d. Some local ladies supplied the music for the silent films. After the opening of the Wardona in 1938, business declined. During the Second World War the building was used for dances and socials. Eventually it became the Roman Catholic Church. The Roman Catholics had previously held occasional services at the Institute.

At different times the basement was turned into a restaurant and also a barber's.

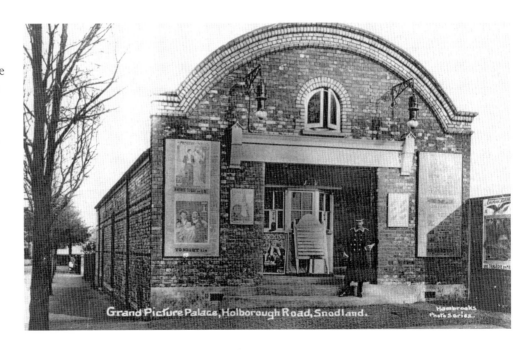

36 This photograph of Holborough Road was taken in 1926, shortly before it was widened. On the right, looking rather decrepit among the trees, is Prospect Cottage, once a fifteenth-century hall-house similar to 'Mulberry Cottage' in the High Street. The shell of this remains, but a major brick addition was made around 1780 by Jasper Crothall (d.1781), the owner of the paper mill and of the house at this time. Even before 1800 the south end of the building had become a butcher's shop and remained so until the mid-twentieth century. Four acres of land belonged to the house, which has undergone extensive renovation and rebuilding in recent years. Some of the Victorian houses opposite have been replaced by modern ones. The insurance agent is calling in his Clymo car, while children are making their way to or from the British Schools by the Clock Tower.

THE SCHOOLS, HOLBOROUGH ROAD, SNODLAND.

37 The British Schools were erected in 1857 by the Nonconformists in Snodland, who wished that their children should 'be free from that class of religious instruction usually taught in Church Schools'. In the early days the schools were poorly managed, but they were purchased by Charles Townsend Hook in 1873 and placed on a secure and successful footing. In 1877-1878 the clock tower was erected as a memorial to him by his mother and sisters as the plaque on it reminds us. By 1888 numbers had grown to such an extent that the adjacent Congregational Chapel was purchased to house the infant department, the Congregationalists moving to their new chapel in the High Street. The school continued to flourish until 1930, when Snodland Central School was opened, followed by St. Katherine's County Primary School on 30 May 1932. In later years the buildings were used for a variety of purposes – a film studio, a glass-blowing factory, basket making and printing. The fine clock tower is all that remains today, with houses built on the rest of the site.

38 The 'Prince of Wales' pub, together with the adjacent 'Prince of Wales Terrace' was built in the 1860s, at a time when the future Edward VII assumed many public duties following the death of his father. As it happens he was a friend of the Roberts family of Holborough and on at least one occasion the school children were allowed out to line the street to cheer him as he passed by. The building was demolished in the early 1980s to make way for the by-pass. This scene evidently dates from around 1910: Masons, the photographers, were active for a few years in the early 1900s. Quite possibly the occasion was the coronation of George V, for the flags over the road seem to indicate a special event. We can be fairly sure that the 'Ten Little Niggers' were part of an entertainment organized by the Working Men's Club, where they made frequent appearances.

39   John May (1734-1805) is remembered today as the creator of two charities dated 10 October 1800: one provided for the education of forty poor children (twenty from Snodland and ten each from Halling and Birling) at what became the National Schools in Brook Street; the other granted £20 a year to provide greatcoats for poor persons in the same three parishes. The former scheme became redundant, but the latter still allocates warm clothing to needy parishioners. This portrait once labelled 'Mr. May of Holborough' was presented to the parish council in 1896 by Humphrey Wood of Chatham, who recorded that before 1878 it belonged to John Lewis Ling of Rochester and was acquired from his estate. It now hangs in the Medway Room at the Devonshire Rooms.

40　We know that Agnes Hook (1846-1903) was an amateur artist, but only two of her water-colour paintings are known to have survived, although there are rough twentieth-century copies of three others which were probably by her. The 'Farm Cottage, Holborough Road' of this mid-nineteenth-century view is Covey Hall farmhouse. In 1881 Joseph Champion rebuilt the house to its present state, although some of the old framework was retained. The earliest reference to the name currently known dates from 1817. This was from ancient times one of the main farms in the parish, but during the twentieth century the growth of the village and later the extraction of clay and chalk for cement encroached upon the land and it became unviable.

41   Here is another of Agnes Hook's paintings, this time looking west up the High Street from a point beside the present Waghorn Road. Its contemporary caption reads 'Snodland, 1864. Left-hand cottages – site of the Church of the New Jerusalem, 1882'. One of these housed the first post office in the village. Those on the right survived much longer, but eventually fell victim to the need for road widening around 1970. They were known as 'Gorham's Cottages' and were built around 1800 by William Gorham (1759-1820), uncle to Snodland's most famous resident, Thomas Fletcher Waghorn. (Gorham married Mary Fletcher, whose father previously owned the land.) According to the overseer's accounts, the house on the extreme right was converted from a stable around 1838.

42 The tithe map of 1844 shows the hamlet of Holborough to have been about as large as Snodland at that time. Today, all that remains can be seen in this photograph of about 1905. 'Little Holborough', or 'Mill Stream Cottage' is in the foreground, with 'Island Cottage' and the water mill behind. The old road to Rochester forded the stream and turned past the mill to rejoin the present route at the Halling boundary. The stream has some of the purest water in the district and according to Edward Hasted, the Kent historian, plans were made by Sir John Marsham and Sir Charles Bickerstaff to pipe it to the Medway towns 'by a cut or channel through Halling and Cuxton thither, four miles of which was through Sir John Marsham's own lands, but after they had proceeded two miles, finding some obstructions, which could not be removed, but by an act, this was procured for the purpose in the 1st year of James II (1685), but nothing further was afterwards done for it.'

HOLBOROUGH MILL, SNODLAND, KENT

43   The building in the centre of this photograph of about 1907 is actually 'Island Cottage', with just part of the water mill visible on the right. The latter is mentioned in the first charter of Snodland, dated 838 A.D., but probably a forgery made by the monks of Rochester a hundred years or so later. From at least the time of the Norman Conquest the mill belonged to the Bishop of Rochester, who leased it to others, who in turn leased it to the millers. It was extensively rebuilt to its present form in 1881, but ceased operations by the turn of the century. 'Island Cottage' may at first have been 'the litle mesuage and garden at Holberth ... nowe devided into twoe dwellinges' which William Tilghman set up as an almshouse in his will of 1593. Between 1827 and her death in 1859, it was the home of Ann, mother of Thomas Fletcher Waghorn. In 1834 he married Harriet Martin, daughter of the miller next door.

Holboro Mill, Snodland

44 Snodland had no resident aristocratic family with extensive estates like the Nevill family in neighbouring Birling. Nevertheless the Holborough estate was of 150 acres and the wealthiest parishioners farmed it. In 1846 it was bought by William Lee when he set up his lime works nearby. His grandson, William Henry Roberts (1848-1926), who lived at Birling at the time, came into possession of it in 1881. He decided to pull down the main house (then about 100 years old) and build new on a site a little further to the north. The result was this imposing building called 'Holborough Court', which we are told incorporated 'a considerable amount of the materials' from the old house. This is an artist's impression, based on the design by Hubert Bensted.

45 This view of Holborough Court shows the rear of the house. William Henry Roberts had Birling House in Birling built for him in 1876, but moved to Holborough Court when it was ready in 1885. He was Major and Hon. Lieutenant-Colonel of the Royal West Kent Regiment and was a keen yachtsman, being a member of the Royal Yacht Squadron, Cowes. He was also a friend of the Prince of Wales (later Edward VII), so the house saw much social activity when he was resident there and the polo field on the estate was in frequent use. Between 1914 and 1920 his son took over and it briefly became the home of his nephew John Cooke Roberts in 1931, but the house was demolished the following year after APCM had bought the estate.

Holborough Court.

46 Here in 1878 are four generations of one family. Seated on the left is William Lee (1803-1881), owner of lime works at Halling from 1846, Liberal MP for Maidstone during most years between 1853 and 1870, Deputy Lieutenant of Kent, a magistrate, Bridgewarden at Rochester, and a churchwarden at Snodland. Opposite him is his daughter Anne (1823-1881), who married William Henry Roberts (1817-1848). Her husband died within a year or so of their marriage. She was a great benefactor to All Saints' Church. Their son William Henry Roberts (1848-1926) – standing – took over management of his grandfather's works from 1881 to 1912, when they were acquired by BPCM. His son William Lee Henry Roberts (1871-1928) founded Holborough Cement Co. Ltd. in 1923 at a new site at Holborough. This was acquired in 1931 by APCM (now Blue Circle) and closed in 1984, but there are plans to develop a new works there.

47 After he had moved to Holborough, William Lee evidently disliked the fact that the road passed so near his house. On 25 March 1850 the Trustees of the Toll Road from Strood to Malling agreed to a proposal for an improvement at Holborough 'by making the Road thro' the Blacksmith's Forge (literally!) and across the Field in front of Mr. Lee's residence'. The agreement was conditional on William Lee paying for it himself; the Trustees had insufficient funds to make the alteration, but were prepared to maintain it thereafter. This view shows the new route as it looked until the enlargements required by the by-pass transformed it in 1983. William Lee's long wall has been reinstated and the gatehouse remains, but not the impressive gates. The gatehouse was for many years the home of gardeners on the estate. The driveway, built in 1850, was further extended when the new house was built in 1884.

Holborough Road, Snodland

48   At the Snodland-Halling boundary a railway track ran across the main road from Lee's works into the chalk pits, which still remains to this day. Since there were no protecting gates someone had to be on hand to control the traffic. In May 1977 Ida K. Raven, born at the 'Cedars' nearby in 1886 and whose father was manager of the works, described what she remembered: 'Sid Coulter used to stand with a large red flag to warn the traffic of oncoming danger when the load of trucks 8 to 10 came hurtling down from the chalk pits, great lumps of chalk piled high in each truck – a splendid little engine gallantly pulled all the empty trucks up to the pits again & so it went on except for Sunday. ...' In 1905, when this picture was taken, there can have been virtually no motor traffic, but those driving a horse and cart needed to be on their guard.

Holborough Rd, Snodland, Kent

49   Queen's Road and Queen's Avenue were of course named after Queen Victoria, but both date from the very last years of her reign. Just the east part of Queen's Road appears on the 1897 Ordnance Survey map, but nothing of Queen's Avenue. However, Alexandra Terrace is dated 1901 and other houses were built the following year. In 1905 the builder Joshua Wilford was still giving his address as 'Sunnyside' in Church Fields, but by 1909 he was using these premises in Queen's Avenue (now named Lambert Mews after a later owner). In the photograph he is second from the left.

As well as his building work, he was undertaker, funeral provider and monumental mason and also 'contractor to the Malling Union' (where the destitute of local parishes were sent following the Poor Reform Act of 1834) in these services.

50   Here is Joshua Wilford again, in 1919, at his final house. This is 'The Lodge' in the upper High Street, built by Thomas Fletcher Waghorn (1800-1850) around 1841. Waghorn's parents were married at All Saints' Church, but they lived in Chatham, where all their ten children were born. Waghorn joined the Royal Navy aged twelve. Between 1820 and 1831 he served in the Bengal Pilot Service of the East India Company. He made it his life's work to devise more rapid communications between India and England. In the mid-1830s he set up a route through the Egyptian desert, making use of the new steamships which traversed the Red Sea.

A combination of bad luck (plague killing his horses) and government indifference plunged him into debt in his last years and the route was taken over by others. He died in London, but is buried at All Saints', where there is also a tablet to his memory. The Lodge is now a residential home, but retains features from Waghorn's time, including a door in which is inserted a panel he acquired when in India.

51 This snowy scene shows 'Dodnor Cottages', formerly beside the junction between Birling Road and the Paddlesworth Road (next to the 'Monk's Head'). The origin of the name 'Dodnor' has not been discovered. Originally this was a large fifteenth-century property called Benet's Place, presumably built by Thomas Benet (d. 1461), one of the principal landowners at the time. In his will he also gave money towards the building of the west porch at All Saints' Church. Around 1820 Benet's Place was bought by Thomas Stephens, the farmer at Paddlesworth, who converted the L-shaped building into four cottages for his farm labourers. Each was allocated part of the adjacent land for a garden. 'Dodnor Cottages' were demolished in the 1970s and new houses now occupy the site.

52   One of the oldest known photographs of Snodland is this one of Woodlands farmhouse in 1867. It clearly matches a drawing from the 1820s made by the Kent artist William Twopeny, now among the collection of his works in the Department of Prints and Drawings at the British Museum. The farm is of great antiquity; some seventeenth-century deeds refer to it as 'Newhouse', implying that an earlier building once occupied the site. Like much of Snodland it came into the hands of the Earls of Romney during the seventeenth century and was sold for £4,000 to William Gorham in 1808. Between 1820 and 1879 it belonged to the Luck family of West Malling.

53   This picture shows Woodlands farmhouse in the 1930s. It is clear when comparisons are made with the previous picture that much was altered when Joseph Champion, the new owner, rebuilt it in 1881. So much has changed, indeed, that one wonders how much of the original building was retained. The present wing on the right is entirely a nineteenth-century addition – part of Champion's rebuild – and the earlier one seems to have disappeared. Elsewhere a single storey has become two and a cottage has been added on the left. Much of the farm land belonging to Woodlands has been lost to housing or to clay and chalk extraction.

Woodlands, Snodland, Kent.

A. N. Hambrooks
Photo Series.

54 The view in this picture is towards the south-east and dates from around 1908. Snodland Cemetery was opened in 1896 (with the first burial on 19 March). The gatehouse and chapel were designed by Hubert Bensted of Maidstone (who earlier had designed Holborough Court). The cemetery has since been extended on the south side. In the foreground is the ruin of 'Coney Hall' – so called in a map of 1740 – which was part of the estate belonging to Covey Hall farm. At one time the property seems to have served as the dower house to the farm (for the use of the widow when the farmer died and the son took over), but in later years was occupied by farm labourers. The ruin was finally destroyed by chalk excavation in the mid-twentieth-century.

Snodland Cemetery, from "the Knob"

55 'The Knob' was a chalk hill separate from the North Downs behind it. Quite possibly ancient man viewed it as a special feature, for at its summit (210 feet) was placed a Bronze Age barrow. Later a Roman tumulus was added a few yards to the north and later still, about 650-750 A.D., a Saxon cemetery was made between the two barrows. These features were all excavated in the 1950s and 1960s before the entire hill was eaten up by chalk extraction. Among the important finds were Saxon weaponry and a Roman chair, a decorated child's lead coffin and a purse. Alongside these burials was an ancient trackway, running along the foot of the North Downs at the spring-line, through Trottiscliffe and Paddlesworth, but here deviating towards the river and a crossing at Holbor-ough. In the picture smoke from the chimneys at Peters' lime and cement works (said to have been the largest of its kind) can be seen.

56 Those who drive through Snodland on the main road would be surprised to know that a large part of the parish comprises beautiful countryside, even though the town continues to encroach upon it. The westernmost end of the parish is covered by part of the North Downs. Running at the foot of the hills is the ancient trackway, which the Victorians called 'The Pilgrim's Road'. Certainly pilgrims from Winchester to the shrine of Thomas à Becket at Canterbury would have travelled this way, but the road is much older than that. Some would continue on the Rochester to cross the Med-way there, while others could deviate through Snodland, where a river crossing could also be made.

The Hills & Pilgrim's Way, Snodland.

HAMBROOK'S PHOTO SERIES.

57　The hamlet of Paddlesworth comprises a farm and a church and it is unlikely that the scene changed much over the last thousand years until recent additions of modern buildings and tarmacadam roads. Since 1888 it has been part of the parish of Snodland, for the little Norman church reminds us that once this was a separate parish with its own rector. In 1366 the parish of Dode (over the hill) was joined to it, because the population there supposedly perished in the Black Death. One rector served both until Henry VIII seized his stipend. In the seventeenth century it became a farm outhouse and remained so until 1933, when John Cooke Roberts of Holborough restored it as a private chapel. In 1951 it was bought by the Bishop of Rochester and in recent years was purchased for the nation by the Churches Conservation Trust, who now care for it. It is open at weekends and services are held at Harvest and Christmas.

OLD CHURCH, PADDLESWORTH, SNODLAND.

58 The large farmhouse at Paddlesworth on the right of this photograph is believed to have been built around 1690-1700 by George Wray (d.1713). The red-brick building to the fore is rather later (about 1750), although it has some older features. The date of the picture is unknown, but it was taken before 1930, when the small extension to the main house (on the extreme right) was demolished. Out of sight to the right is a fifteenth-century barn, which, to judge by an inventory of 1570, must have been the farmhouse prior to George Wray's building. The pond has disappeared, as has the barn on the left. Today a modern farmhouse replaces Wray's, although the latter survives as a store and has seen some restoration.

59   Malling Road is the main route into Snodland from the south and is always busy. Yet until it was authorized in 1825-1826 anyone journeying towards Leybourne and Malling would have had to follow a roundabout route via Birling Road and Hollow Lane. This straight cut from the 'Bull' Hotel to Ham Hill was part of a toll road. The toll keeper would collect his money from a little house where the Medway Bakery is today. It was not until the 1870s that houses began to line the street, initially as far as Chapel Road and the path which today is replaced by Rocfort Road. Here in 1873, in a hopfield, PC Israel May was murdered by a drunken man – the first policeman in Kent to have been killed on duty. The event shocked the whole nation. Baldock's shop, seen here in this 1912 photograph, served the community for 110 years until its closure in 2000. On the other side of Bramley Road is L. Wraight, a saddler and harness-maker, who moved to Holborough Road in 1913.

Malling Road, Snodland. (3).

Hambrook's Photo Series.

60 This busy scene is a little further south than the previous picture and was captured by William Bateman around 1906-1909. Christian Pries opened his general stores in 1906, but the building is rather earlier – it still has a Victorian postbox attached to it. Here a tradesman is about to make a delivery to him. Perhaps the steam-roller was made by the nearby Rochester firm of Aveling and Porter. A horse and cart pulls away from outside Charles Brattle's painter's and decorator's shop. On the far side of this is Tudor House, built in 1888 for Mr. Thornhill's private school. It later became the home of the Salvation Army and is now private dwellings. All the other houses date from the 1880s and 1890s.

SNODLAND, KENT.   MALLING ROAD.   W. BATEMAN, POST OFFICE, SNODLAND.

61 This picture was taken from virtually the same place as the previous one, but facing south rather than north. Only about a dozen of these houses are shown on the 1897 Ordnance Survey map, but most have sprung up in the ten years or so before this picture was taken in about 1909. Among the new properties are those set back on the left – Raymead Villas and Sillwood Place. No footpath yet exists on this side of the road – it was added in 1910. On 5 August 1944 a flying bomb landed on this area, causing wide-spread damage, injury and loss of life. Several houses were demolished, including the Manse for the Congregational Church, and new ones now take their place.

62   On 11 June 1892 'The Birling Building Estate' sold 34 plots of land on either side of Malling Road. These were part of an estate which formerly had belonged to Walter Coulson and in 1862 were given in part of a marriage settlement to his son Rev. Thomas Borlase Coulson. It was intended that most of the plots would have two houses built on them, with one or two larger plots allowing terraces (such as Raymead Villas and Sillwood Place). 'Woodbank' (now demolished) and 'Woodcroft' were single larger houses in their respective plots. Construction was piecemeal and this photograph from the early 1900s still shows some gaps which were not filled until later.

Malling Road, Snodland. (1).

63   Originally Bull Field was probably the field where the village's bull was kept – and from which in turn it is likely that the 'Old Bull' and 'Bull Hotel' received their names. The increasing demands for workers as the cement and paper factories grew led to a corresponding requirement for houses for them. In 1868 Bull Field was just that – a field, but during the 1870s it was completely covered by houses and gardens. Twelve shops were added in the upper High Street, 24 houses and the Primitive Methodist Chapel in Malling Road, 14 houses in 'Bottom Row' (Chapel Road) and 28 houses in Portland Place – all on what was 'Bull Field'. A note on the reverse of this photograph identifies it as Portland Place around 1910, but the reason for the gathering of children is unknown. Perhaps an outing was planned.

64 A large part of what is now the southern part of Snodland (formerly in Birling parish) came into the possession of Walter Coulson and in 1862 he willed it to his son, the Rev. Thomas Borlase Coulson, as part of his marriage settlement. In time Thomas' widow and daughters sold the estate piece by piece. Most of this land was attached to Rookery Farm. Bramley Road is supposedly named after the birthplace of Thomas. This may be so – certainly a Coulson family is well established there in the nineteenth century – but Thomas has proved difficult to trace. In fact Bramley Road had no name at the time of the 1891 census and by 1897 only about half of the houses in this photograph of about 1910 had been completed. Thomas Coulson himself died in 1895, so if he did name the road it was late in life.

BRAMLEY ROAD SNODLAND

65 Although labelled 'Bramley Road' in this early twentieth-century photograph, today this section is called Recreation Avenue, with Bramley Road proper leading off to the right. (The adjacent recreation ground was purchased by the Parish Council in 1924.) Many roads at this time had no tarmacadam surface and in the summer a cart went round spraying water to prevent too much dust. One of the multitude of small corner shops, now sadly gone, can be seen (there was another on the corner with Birling Road in the distance). Here too are some of the forty houses on Birling Road, built in the 1860s by Charles Townsend Hook for workers in his expanding paper mill. Opposite were allotments, today replaced by Charles Close.

66 This pastoral scene of the 1950s is looking west from the bottom of Rookery Hill. Cows are ambling up the hill towards Rookery Farm for milking. The farm was soon to be demolished and in the 1960s 184 houses and bungalows were built on these and adjacent fields to make the Rookery Farm Estate. At the time of building they cost around £3000 freehold. Today Roberts Road runs across the right of this picture, with Roberts Road school (transferred from Brook Street) situated near the gap in the hedge at the back of the field. Directly ahead would be the bungalows on the hill itself, with Taylor Road and Godden Road behind.

67 This old house stood on St. Catherine's Bank (Catherine with a 'C' not a 'K'!) at the east end of St. Katherine's Lane. The road was still called 'Bedlam Lane' as late as 1937 and it is possible that this isolated home had housed imbeciles at some point. It seems to have dated from the late sixteenth century and stood in three-quarters of an acre of land. It was thatched until 1932, but this was replaced by a tin roof. The walls were of brick between the beams with three rooms downstairs and two up. From at least 1690 to 1820 it belonged to the Fletcher family (from which Thomas Fletcher Waghorn received his middle name). The house was demolished in 1974 and bungalows now occupy the site.

68   On the Birling-Snodland border stood Grove Farm, evidently one of the oldest in the neighbourhood. Its situation caused friction between Birling and Snodland, both of whom claimed it as part of their respective parishes. This was officially resolved on 21 November 1693 when Snodland paid Birling £4 10s. and Birling in turn allowed that Grove Farm should henceforth be part of Snodland parish. It is ironic then that the farm continued to be listed in Birling in all the censuses to 1891! One farmhouse on the site is known to have been pulled down in the late eighteenth century and the last one was demolished in the 1950s. Houses in 'The Groves' seen in this early twentieth-century photograph still line the road nearby.

BIRLING ROAD NEAR SNODLAND

69   Snodland Central School was opened on 19 May 1930 and it is likely that this photograph was taken around then. It was regarded as a showpiece building when it opened and had 293 pupils on the first roll. To the school came older pupils from the National Schools in Brook Street and particularly the British Schools in Holborough Road. With the opening of St. Katherine's County Primary School on 30 May 1932 younger pupils were also catered for nearby, so the British Schools closed, as did the little school at Ham Hill. In 1961 the school's name was changed to Holmesdale Secondary Modern School (the 'Modern' was dropped in 1965). Since 1993 it has been called Holmesdale Community School and the site now includes Adult Education facilities added alongside the well-established Youth Service department.

CENTRAL SCHOOL SNODLAND

70   The hamlet of Ham Hill has recently become part of the parish of Snodland. At the time of the 1841 census just seventeen old houses, with a farm and public house were here, mostly lining Brook Lane. Towards the end of the nineteenth century many more were added on the main road. Ham Hill may have been picturesque, but seems to have been rather run-down in those early days. Most of the area is now covered with modern buildings and very few of the old houses remain. One exception is this lovely row of four cottages in Brook Lane, photographed in the 1970s. In 1841 the tenants were William Summerton, John and Mary Smith, Robert and Fanny Allchin and William and Mary Lee.

71   Here part of the funeral procession for Dr. Douglas Freeland enters the cemetery gates on 14 October 1908. Dr. Freeland was son-in-law to Eustace Hook of the paper mill family and lived at Delamere House with his wife Marian Eva. His father John Baker Freeland was also a doctor and had lived with them until his death four years earlier. Douglas was a partner of John Palmer (see picture 15). Unusually the local newspapers do not seem to have reported the funeral in detail, although a notice of Freeland's serious illness before his death does appear. The Snodland photographers R. Mason & Sons advertised a photograph of the funeral the following week: this one is theirs and there is also another of the service at the graveside.

72   In towns and villages throughout the land the creation and unveiling of war memorials followed the ending of the First World War. In Snodland, on 13 June 1920, the unveiling of the cenotaph in the cemetery was carried out by Rear-Admiral Sir Doveton Sturdee. In December 1914, the British Naval squadron from Stanley, under command of Admiral Sturdee, defeated the German fleet at the Battle of the Falkland Islands and thus regained control of the South Atlantic. Here he is presented with an address drawn up for the occasion by the Parish Council. Clearly little traffic was expected in Holborough Road once the admiral's car had arrived. The whole company went in procession to the cemetery for the unveiling ceremony and service, where further photographs were taken.

Presentation of address to Admiral Sturdee. Snodland. June 13th. 1920.

73 The corner of Malling Road and the upper High Street has seen many changes over the years. This photograph dates from 1910. Daniel Chalklen had moved his cycle shop from the corner of Bramley Road in 1908. It is unlikely that he had much trade in motor vehicles at this time. The building still carries its plaque of 'Windham House' and evidently was named by the first resident. He was Robert Jackson, a harness maker from Wymondham (pronounced 'Windham'), Norfolk. Next door was one of the hairdressers in the village – Ernest Baron was the proprietor here in 1915. The Garage has been a shop for very many years. Note that there was no public road here: access to Portland Place and Bull Field was via Chapel Road only.

74 The advent of large (and small) supermarkets has dealt a serious blow to small shopkeepers in communities like Snodland. In 1955 the Women's Institute recorded 68 shops here, including 3 bakers, 5 butchers, 6 drapers, 7 grocers, 6 greengrocers, 10 general stores, 3 shoe-shops and 9 tobacconist/newsagent/confectioners. Stephen Collison, aged 19, a butcher from Headcorn, appears in the 1891 census, lodging in Malling Road. In 1903 he set up his butcher's shop in Malling Road and is pictured here with his staff and a special display – probably for Christmas – in 1912. The shop continued through three generations until it closed in January 1999, to be followed the next year by Woolway's; there are now no independent butchers.

75 Charles William Hinds set up his blacksmith's forge at the turn of the twentieth century and it was continued in time by his son Frederick. With car replacing horse as the normal mode of transport, it is appropriate that the Central Garage occupies the site of the forge today.

Both Charles and Frederick were captains of the village Fire Brigade for very many years, which until the Second World War was controlled by the Parish Council. Part of the 'Fireman' notice can be seen on this picture of 'Delhi', Mr. Hinds' house. This was in Malling Road, but was demolished in the 1980s when Rocfort Road was built, replacing what was formerly just a footpath.

C.W.HINDS, R.S.S. Shoeing & General Smith, Wheelwright & Coachbuilder, Malling Road, Snodland.

76 Punish farm is high on the downs at the west of the parish. It is believed that it takes its name from the Povenasshe family, documented here between 1242 and 1346. During the sixteenth and seventeenth centuries Punish was held in turn by a family called Browne and then by the Dalison family of Halling. Between 1653 and 1808 it passed to the Marsham family of Cuxton (the Earls of Romney) and then for many years to William Tidd. In the later nineteenth century the original farmhouse was replaced by this imposing building called 'Holly Hill House' or 'Holly Hill Towers', built and occupied in turn by Thomas Day, William H. Day and Francis H. Cripps Day.